NE̶ ̶CENTURY

Mark Finley
and Steven Mosley

Pacific Press® Publishing Association
Nampa, Idaho
Oshawa, Ontario, Canada

Edited by Tim Lale
Designed by Tim Larson
Cover photo by Ken Reid © FPG International

Copyright © 1999 by
Pacific Press® Publishing Association
Printed in the United States of America
All rights reserved

ISBN 0-8163-1762-3

99 00 01 02 03 • 5 4 3 2 1

Contents

A Hand in the Future 5

Going to Extremes 15

Can You Protect Your Family? 25

The Ultimate Space Journey 35

Information Overload 45

Preserving You on a Disk 55

A Hand in the Future

What did life in the year 2000 look like—when it was still some distance away?

People predicted all kinds of things: climate-controlled clothing, robots for walking the dog, 3-D videophones on every street corner. We were told that we'd be taking a jet-car to the office for a three-hour workday and, on weekends, get away to the moon.

People vastly over-estimated our ability to manage the environment. The weather would be fine tuned, experts assured us, in cities beneath huge domes. The Sahara would become green and the Antarctic temperate. Sickness, pollution and poverty would be no more than a bad memory.

Well, life at the beginning of a new millennium doesn't look quite like that. We still get the flu and have to fight through freeway traffic on the way to our eight-hour workdays.

So we're still left wondering—will life get significantly better or will it stay about the same? Just what can we count on in the next century?

In 1979, a distinguished panel of experts, appointed by President Jimmy Carter, issued what they called Report of the Year 2000. They'd spent months trying to look into the future; they'd spent a lot of money trying to spot significant trends.

Unfortunately, their report failed to foresee the most important ones. No one guessed that the mighty Soviet Empire would collapse—and radically alter the face of Europe. No one guessed the dramatic effect Asian countries—like Taiwan, South Korea and Malaysia—would suddenly have on the global economy.

In his book, *The Next 500 Years,* Adrian Berry tells us something very interesting. Not a single government forecaster predicted any of the events that have shaped the world after World War II. No one predicted the cold war or the Arab oil embargo of 1973 or the electronics boom that followed the moon landing.

However, that sobering fact didn't stop Adrian Berry himself from trying to look 500 years into the future.

We are curious about what's just around the bend. We are especially curious as we stand on the threshold of a new century, and yes, of a new millennium.

Newsweek magazine reported, in a series called "The Millennium Notebook," that there's a surge of interest in "futurism." It's become a very trendy profession.

One analyst pointed out that, at the end of the last century, it was "Victorian psychics with turbans and crystal balls talking to angels." At the turn of this century, it's data crunchers in office cubicles telling us what lies ahead.

Businesses are hiring more and more futurists as consultants. They want to do long-range planning. They want to jump on trends and get their share of the market. They want to know, for example, if retail stores are going to eventually disappear. Will everyone do their shopping on the Internet in a couple of decades?

And all of us face much bigger questions about the future. Will ethnic conflicts spread all over the world? Will some dictator or terrorist acquire nuclear weapons and start threatening an entire city somewhere with annihilation? Will our environment withstand the wave of technology that is changing countries everywhere?

Above everything else, we want to find hope in the next century. We want some reassurance that a shaky economy or ethnic violence or terrorism or environmental disaster won't overwhelm us.

Is there anything we can count on in the 21st century? Things are changing so rapidly, it's hard to know. The marvelous new computer you buy becomes outdated in less than a year. National boundaries are re-drawn so often that school textbooks can't keep up with them.

And what about the generation coming of age in the 21st century and trying to find a place in society? What kind of world will they need to fit into?

In the Western world, Gen-Xers are pessimistic about their economic future. We've moved from the Industrial Age to the Global Age, and downsizing has become the watchword in one major company after another. Many young people can't find an entry-level job that will enable them to pay back their student loans.

Hope doesn't come easy to the generation that will reach maturity in the 21st century. They are the first generation that has grown up worried they won't live as well as their parents did.

Many of them have watched their families fall apart. They are the children of divorce. They are the grandchildren of the sexual revolution. And they're not sure what they can really believe in.

Earlier generations seemed to have larger-than-life heroes they could cling to. The generation that survived the Depression and won World War II seems, from this distance, to have been so sure of their values.

Then came the Baby Boomer generation, my generation. Many rejected their parents' values in the 60s. Boomers didn't see honesty and hard work; they just saw materialism. They felt the government and the corporate world were the enemy.

And Boomer parents have tended to paint a gloomy picture of all authority and of the future. Underarm deodorants are going to destroy the ozone layer and give us all cancer. Nuclear power will flood the earth with radiation. Some fanatic will kill us all in a nuclear war.

This is what Gen-X kids have grown up hearing from an awful lot of Baby Boomer parents. They know about the problems. They know about society's failures. But what about hope? They don't have any solid values to fall back on. The things you could always count on have leeched away over the years.

How can a new generation find hope in the 21st century? Can we find something that will be there for us in the decades ahead?

Let me make a suggestion. To find hope in the 21st century, we're not looking for some*thing* but for Some*one*. Let's start by looking for Someone who's been there for us in the 20th century and the 19th century and the 18th century.

I'd like to tell you about just such a Person. Let me give you a quick, bird's-eye view of an Individual who's been there for people down through history.

About 3,000 years ago, a young shepherd discovered something during his lonely nights on the hills of Judea. His name was David. He discovered that the God of heaven could extend His hand to Earth. He could be present in a special way.

As David expressed it, "The Lord is my Shepherd, I shall not be in want. He makes me lie down in green pastures."

This young man came to know that God's hand was there with him, whether he was fighting off lions and bears or fleeing from a jealous King Saul. God's hand was always with him.

Hundreds of years later, a prophet named Isaiah faced a crisis. Mighty Assyria was threatening his homeland, tiny Israel, with total destruction.

But Isaiah discovered that "The Lord is the Rock eternal," and he was able to testify with these words: "You will keep in perfect peace him whose mind is steadfast, because he trusts in you" (Isaiah 26:3, 4, NIV).

Fast forward to A.D. 54. A prisoner named Paul wrote a letter to friends in Philippi. He was awaiting word on his sentence; Roman authorities could have condemned him to death. But in this difficult situation, Paul the apostle felt that God was present.

In fact, his letter to the Philippians flows with love and encouragement. He keeps telling believers to rejoice in the Lord always. And, in his chains, he recommends the peace of God that surpasses all understanding.

Move on through the centuries to the year 1497. A terrible plague had swept through the city of Florence. Many were dying. But in the midst of this fearful pestilence, a preacher named Savonarola, who was organizing the efforts to help the sick, witnessed something remarkable. Many people responded with love instead of panic. Savonarola wrote: "The citizens here are so full of charity that they have given us their palaces and paid all our expenses."

Florence had experienced something of a revival under the influence of Savonarola's powerful preaching. They wanted God to become a real force in their lives. And now they were experiencing that presence—in the worst of times.

Even Savonarola was filled with wonder. He said, "It is quite unbelievable how joyful are the spirits of those who believe, in life as well as in death."

During the 1980s, Peter Rumachik endured great hardships, locked up in a harsh prison in the Soviet Gulag. Because he refused to renounce his Christian faith, Peter was often placed in punishment cells or kept in solitary confinement. Confined by iron and concrete, suffering cold and hunger, he became so sick on several occasions that he could barely breathe.

No one thought the man could survive. This was his fifth imprisonment for preaching the gospel. Peter was a gifted speaker, and the authorities wanted him silenced.

But this pastor's spirit couldn't keep quiet. The other men in neighboring cells began to hear the most unexpected sound coming from Peter's dark, dank cell. He was singing hymns. He was lifting up praises to God.

After a bit, Peter stopped and called out, "Do you want me to sing some more?"

The others replied in awe, "Yes, if you have strength, sing some more."

And so Pastor Rumachik's voice continued echoing through the prison. The thieves, murderers, and rapists around him had never heard words like these. Peter sang hour after hour as they listened, enraptured.

He was singing because God's hand was there with him in that terrible place. He was singing because, as he put it, "My heart enjoyed the presence of God."

And before Peter's unexpected release in 1987, he had led several fellow prisoners to repentance and faith in Jesus Christ.

God's hand stretches from century to century. It touches people in every place, in every situation. It gives us peace and hope.

The foundation of hope in the 21st century is this: God's hand stretches into the future. The Almighty can touch our lives in the decades ahead. That's why we can have hope. We can have hope because God has a plan.

The writers of Scripture tell us over and over that God's right hand holds us up, that God's right hand lifts us high, that God covers us with the shadow of His hand, that we can become a royal diadem in His hand.

In fact, one psalmist gives us this wonderful picture: "You open Your hand and satisfy the desire of every living thing" (Psalm 145:16, NKJV).

This is the hand that is stretched into the future, into the 21st century. As the prophet Isaiah assures us: "His hand is stretched out, and who will turn it back" (Isaiah 14:27).

The psalmist went through a period of anguish and perplexity. But in this dark time, he did find one important answer. This is what he discovered: "I am continually with You; You hold me by my right hand. You will guide me with Your counsel, and afterward receive me to glory" (Psalm 73:23, 24, NKJV).

In Psalm 139, we find the same belief expressed in a different way. Verse 10 expresses the psalmist's assurance of what he could always count on: "If I ascend into heaven, You are there; if I make my bed in hell, behold, You are there. If I take the wings of the morning, and dwell in the uttermost parts of the sea, even there Your hand shall lead me, and Your right hand shall hold me" (Psalm 139:8-10, NKJV).

God's hand stretches out to us no matter where we are. And it stretches out into the future. It will be there to care for us. That's why we can have hope no matter what happens in the next millennium.

And there's something very important you need to understand about that hand, the hand of God. It doesn't just move events in general; it's not just nudging the big picture here and there. The hand of God touches individual lives; it touches your life. And it will touch individuals in the new century.

The Bible expresses this fact with a very interesting symbol. It pictures God as a farmer, as a vinedresser. In Psalm 80, we see Him planting a choice vine, preparing room for it and making it take deep root so that it fills the land.

Isaiah pictures God cultivating a vineyard on a very fruitful hill: "He dug it up and cleared out its stones, and planted it with the choicest vine. He built a tower in its midst" (Isaiah 5:2, NKJV).

Through the prophet Jeremiah we get a picture of God carefully cultivating a seed of highest quality to produce a noble vine.

Ezekiel tells a parable about God planting a vineyard in a

garden terrace: "It was planted in good soil by many waters, to bring forth branches, bear fruit, and become a majestic vine" (Ezekiel 17:8, NKJV).

Why do so many Bible writers give us this picture of God the Vinedresser, God getting His hands dirty?

Because they want us to understand how much He invests in each individual. He's not just a farmer-for-hire trying to get a quantity of crop from a certain number of acres. No, He's bent over this one vine; He's digging up the soil around it, watering it, caring for it, making sure it becomes fruitful.

It's interesting to note that in agriculture there's a trend toward what is called "precision farming." That's what's coming in the 21st century. It's a system of crop management based on the idea that no two clumps of dirt are alike. In the past, farming has treated a whole tract of land, basically, as one batch of potting soil. As a result, some areas get too much fertilizer or not enough herbicide.

But precision farming gives a much better picture of what each bit of land needs. It uses satellites, computer mapping systems, and even crop monitors that "read" a plant's health through a beam of light.

Farmers are able to tell exactly where there's a sandy patch, exactly where there's a stand of Russian thistle, and exactly where there's a shortage of phosphorus in the soil.

As a result, they can deliver much more personalized attention. Computers in a tractor, for example, can determine just how much fertilizer to apply to a field. As one farmer said, it's like spoon feeding each plant based on what it needs.

Well, the prophets of the Old Testament anticipated precision farming by a few thousand years. And that's because they were talking about the hand of the Lord, the Vinedresser. He delivers individualized attention. He's not just concerned about the whole crop. He cares for each individual vine, as if it were the only plant in His care.

The hand of God extends into the next century; it extends

into the soil of the next century where you will grow. God's hand is there, getting involved, getting dirty. And God's hand has a green thumb.

This is the Great Provider, the One who makes a feast appear in the desert, a spring gush from solid rock, and the "bread of angels" fall from the sky. He can even spread a table for us in the presence of our enemies.

He leads us, as David discovered, through green pastures beside quiet waters. Because of His attentions, the meadows are covered with flocks and the valleys are mantled with grain.

God wants to be your Provider in the next century. God wants to open His hand and satisfy your deepest desires.

In this book, we'll be talking about how God can help us meet the specific challenges of a new century. We'll be discovering how His principles can help us thrive amid the changes that the decades ahead will bring.

But everything starts with this foundation of hope, with this basic fact: God's hand extends into the future. It's a hand that blesses us. It's a hand that can touch us individually.

The hand of the Father is revealed in the hand of Christ. It was the hand of Christ that healed lepers and gave sight to the blind. It was the hand of Christ that pulled Peter from a stormy sea and beckoned Lazarus from a cold tomb. It was the hand of Christ that multiplied bread for the hungry multitude. It was the hand of Christ that was nailed to the cross.

It's the hand of Christ that is reaching out to you today. Are you prepared to reach back? Are you prepared to touch God's hand in the 21st century?

You can have a foundation of hope for the future. It's available from the One whose hand heals and nurtures and empowers and loves.

Are you willing to put your hand in His? Are you willing to be cultivated, to be nurtured by this God? Will you open your life to Him right now, so that the one Person who has been there for us in every century, can be there for you in the next?

Going to Extremes

It's the new wave in sports going to extremes, pushing things to the limit, and facing ever greater dangers. A whole new generation is caught up in the momentum of "Extreme Sports." They even have their own Olympics, the X-Games.

And it makes us wonder, how far will people push the limits as we enter a new century? How much further can they go? And what do these new extremes say about what's going on deep inside us?

They usually start out in the darkness before dawn. They have to scale barbed-wire fences, creep up stairwells, and climb high ladders and girders.

Their goal is elevation. They have to find a way to get to the top of a skyscraper or radio tower. These are BASE jumpers, thrill seekers who risk arrest to reach some forbidden precipice. And then, they jump out into thin air, free-fall at 100 miles per hour, and toss out a parachute a few seconds before smashing into the earth.

It's quite an adrenaline rush. But BASE jumpers are just one of a new breed of sports enthusiasts who push things to the extreme.

There are the bungee jumpers, of course. They're always in search of some higher bridge or archway to dive off of. They love the thrill of plummeting to what seems certain death, and then, just a few feet from impact, bouncing back up into the air.

Skiers are no longer content to conquer the deep powder on a steep slope. Now, they must actually ski off rocky cliffs, plummet 50 or 60 feet down a precipice, and then try to keep going on the steep slope below.

Extreme skiing and snowboarding keeps your heart in your throat. But that's the thrill, that's the adrenaline rush that's sweeping a whole new generation into the next century.

They jump out of airplanes, feet attached to boards, and perform incredible acrobatic stunts. That's sky surfing.

They jump off dirt mounds, somersault through the air attached to bicycles, and manage to land on the wheels, most of the time.

Extreme sports are about bigger thrills and bigger spills. And even couch potatoes want a bigger kick, a more vivid sensation. Spectators are demanding more and more extremes in sports and entertainment.

Witness the incredible boom in Pro Wrestling. It's huge on cable TV. On one recent Monday night, as many young men watched Pro Wrestling on TV, as watched the World Series. It has become a whole industry, generating more than one billion dollars a year in the United States, from ticket sales, pay-per-view events, T-shirts, video games and action figures.

But what's especially disturbing is what all the fans, many of them young boys, are screaming and cheering about today. The violence, even though it's faked, has been pushed to extremes. Now they're acting out torture and dismemberment. Sex and sexual assault are now part of the game. Some of the biggest stars are wrestlers who pretend to be psychopaths. And they hear fans telling them, "I wish I could be like that, not give a rip about anyone."

We're moving to extremes in entertainment as we move into a new century. The Millennium Notebook series in *Newsweek* magazine described the new wave in theme parks with this headline: "The Theme Is Extreme." Operators can't build parks fast enough to meet the demand for more and more intense experiences—like walking through a wall of fire. With improved holography and heat blowers, would-be daredevils will be able to feel like they're doing just that.

What does all this tell us about where we're going in the 21st century? Why do we keep pushing the limits?

Well, there's a certain amount of youthful exuberance that will always challenge the limits. Kids have a lot of energy; every new generation seeks a new way to express itself.

And sometimes they create incredibly beautiful new sports. Some of the acrobatics of sky surfers, for example, as they twirl against the far horizon, are spectacular.

But there's also a more ominous theme that echoes under all the new thrill seeking. Sometimes we're pushed to so many extremes because there's so little going on inside us. Sometimes people have to have an adrenaline rush because they don't want to feel the pain and emptiness inside.

Let me give you an example. Marta has been BASE jumping for 10 years. After plummeting off a 1250-foot antenna tower in Florida—and surviving, she had this to say: "I couldn't live without it. I would die inside. In a way, it's not a choice. I need it, to keep happy."

Are more and more people seeking extremes in entertainment because more and more people need it to be happy?

That's a sobering thought. People who keep running are usually running *away* from something. And those who keep running from one thrill to another are no exception.

A French poet once described the human predicament in a way that pictures a lot of what's happening today. He wrote: "Always driven toward new shores, or carried hence without hope of return, shall we never, on the ocean of age, cast anchor for even a day?"

We are restless; we can't find a place to cast anchor, because we're trying to fill the emptiness in our hearts, because we can't find a center for our lives. We're in limbo.

The Bible calls this "The Fall, the fall from grace." Human beings are separated from God their Creator. We have slipped from our natural place of fellowship with God.

It started with Lucifer, an angel in heaven who began to challenge God's authority. He enjoyed one of the highest positions in heaven, near the throne of the Almighty.

But he decided he could do it better on his own, without God's guidance. So he took a very big leap. And what's more, he persuaded many angels to take the plunge with him.

Well, guess what? They discovered that they didn't have parachutes. They just kept plummeting down. There wasn't any safe landing outside of God's plan. So they crashed—they crashed on planet Earth.

And this is where Satan has stubbornly persisted in carrying out his plan of rebellion against God. In the Garden of Eden, he persuaded Adam and Eve to take a chance, to take the leap, and they did. And human beings have been jumping off the cliff and crashing ever since.

Look around you, and you'll realize this planet is a crash site. People are driven to extremes. There's always some dictator who manages to whip a nation or ethnic group into a frenzy and wage war on his neighbors. There's always some new horrible crime making the headlines. Ordinary people keep destroying their families and hurting loved ones in spite of themselves, in spite of knowing better. We keep crashing.

We have to get back to that place we jumped *from*. We have to get back to God, to that place with Him where our hearts can find a home.

We will never find peace as long as we keep fleeing from our heavenly Father. We'll never find peace as long as we substitute thrill seeking for soul searching. We'll never find peace as long as we drown out God's voice with the constant noise of extremes.

Let me tell you about one Gen-Xer who managed to stop

the noise, a young man who managed to fill that emptiness.

When Mark Hughes walked into a Pro Wrestling auditorium in 1988, he thought he'd found what he was searching for. The crowd was roaring over the antics of a man inside a mesh-caged platform. Ted Oates was tossing his opponent around like a sack of potatoes. Here, Mark thought, was guts and glory. Here was a way to get the applause he so desperately wanted.

So Mark used his own background as a wrestler in high school to break into the super-hyped world of Pro Wrestling. He trained under Oates, and he paid his dues. Many mornings he'd wake up with bruises from the previous night's pounding.

But Mark beefed up, often eating six heavy meals a day, and improved his skills. Soon he was winning matches. Promoters billed him as "Marvelous Mark Hughes—Totally Irresistible." Teenagers asked for his autograph. His hometown in Georgia cheered him as a champion. Girls idolized him.

Mark had arrived. But deep inside he knew that his wild capers on the Pro Wrestling stage were really a cover for the turmoil within. He couldn't shake a sense that he just didn't belong. That feeling had started when he was in the sixth grade. In one week his grandfather died, his parents divorced, his two older brothers joined the army, and his sister left home.

Ever since then, Mark had struggled to find a place to "cast anchor." His Marvelous Mark Hughes image gave him a way to direct his energies and gain approval. But many nights after his matches, he'd walk outside, look up at the stars and know there had to be something better.

He also saw more and more of Pro Wrestling's ugly side. One night after a match, an adoring teenager came up and told him she planned to beat up another girl who wasn't his fan. She was trying to impress Mark.

He began to think about the things that his career seemed to encourage. He began to think about the role models these kids were following so devotedly.

Mark felt an urge to find out about the only Being who really deserves our devotion. He began reading the Bible. He studied the Gospels and was deeply moved by Christ's life and death. Here was a Man of peace who had an incredible impact on people's lives.

One day, Mark ran across a verse in Colossians that pushed him toward a commitment. It described the treasures of wisdom and knowledge that are hidden in Christ. Mark knelt down and told God that's what he wanted. He wanted to be taught by this wonderful Christ.

Since that day, Mark Hughes has experienced more and more peace in his life. He discovered that he loved talking about his growing faith with others and began an internship as a pastor in Michigan.

Now, instead of yelling bloody threats as he throws opponents around a ring, Mark persuades others with the beauty of Christ's gospel. He's entered another world. And it's a world where he can belong. It's a place where he is loved unconditionally.

I'd like to tell you why Christ can offer peace, a peace that nothing in the world can give, a peace that passes understanding. I'd like to tell you why Christ can offer peace to people stuck on this crash site, why He can offer rest even to those who've been jumping off the cliff for a long time.

He can do that for only one reason—Jesus went to extremes Himself. He went to extraordinary extremes to rescue us as we plunge toward certain spiritual death. He demonstrated for each one of us extremes of endurance that can break the fall, which can reverse that fatal plunge.

Jesus did this for a world of thrill seekers drowning out His grace, for a world filled with the noise of self-indulgence.

Jesus saved us by enduring—in silence. He covered all of our restless noise with silence, a silence that speaks eloquently of amazing grace.

It started in the dead of night. A squad of bored Roman soldiers began abusing a prisoner who was awaiting trial. Jesus seemed a comic figure to them—this former carpenter from Nazareth claiming to be some Messiah, the Savior of the world. The soldiers blindfolded Christ and then took turns punching Him in the face. With each blow, they asked, "Prophesy! Who is it that struck you?"

They wanted to make the prisoner angry. They wanted Him to strike back in some way, to prove that He was just a man like them. And so they scoffed and jeered at Jesus, and they kept tormenting Him, even spitting in His face.

But the bloodied mouth would not open. Jesus wouldn't curse back. He didn't say a word.

He was enduring the worst that callused human beings could do to Him. He was enduring it in silence because He had to suffer the consequences of sin in our place. He had to stop the noise of human cruelty that had been going on for so long.

It continued when He was dragged before the Jewish court, the Sanhedrin. They wanted Him put to death. Many hired witnesses came forward to repeat outrageous accusations against Christ. One claimed that Jesus wanted to destroy the holy temple and rebuild another one in three days.

The high priest stood up indignantly and asked, "Don't you have even one answer to make?"

Mark tells us: "But He kept silent and answered nothing" (Mark 14:61, NKJV).

Christ would not defend Himself. He would accept all the blame that should have fallen on others.

His silence continued the next morning when He was brought before the Roman governor, Pilate. The chief priests began to make all kinds of charges against Him. They made Him out to be a menace to society.

Pilate demanded to know Christ's response to these very serious charges. Matthew tells us: "And He answered him not one word, so that the governor marveled greatly" (Matthew 27:14, NKJV).

Jesus demonstrated the extremes of His endurance for our sake. He wouldn't lash back when Pilate's soldiers jammed a crown of thorns on His head and threw a purple robe on His bloodied shoulders and thrust a reed in His hand. He didn't open His mouth when they knelt before Him in mock allegiance.

He made no protest when the frenzied mob cried out, "Crucify Him! Crucify Him!"

As He hung on the cross with blood seeping from His hands and arms, a group of His religious rivals came up and started jeering: "He saved others, He can't save Himself."

But they couldn't provoke a reply from the Man who had calmed a raging storm with a single command: "Peace, be still."

Soldiers joined in making sport of this odd criminal. One of the thieves crucified beside Him lashed out bitterly, "Aren't you the Christ? Rescue yourself and us!"

But Jesus wouldn't save Himself. He was surrounded by the extremes of human cruelty, people actually making fun of someone who was being tortured to death. But no word of judgment or condemnation came out of His mouth.

Jesus endured it all in silence.

Jesus did speak on occasion during His ordeal at Golgotha. He did utter memorable words when He could extend grace to someone.

But it's His silence that speaks most forcefully about what He was willing to suffer for us. His silence echoes the extremes of Christ's endurance.

He was determined to take the fatal plunge, the ultimate crash, to break our fall. And He endured it all until they took His broken, limp body down from the cross.

Yes, the silence of Christ speaks loudly to us today. It's far more eloquent than all the noise around us. It's what enables Him to extend so much forgiveness and peace. It's enough to fill up a new century.

In Colossians, Paul tells us that our heavenly Father through Christ was able to " . . . reconcile all things to Himself, by Him, . . . having made peace through the blood of His cross" (Colossians 1:20, NKJV).

The cross brings us peace. It takes us back to that place we jumped *from*. It takes us back to reconciliation with God.

Christ created peace in a world where people keep crashing. He created a way for us to find rest—through His silence. In that quietness, we can be still and know God, know that He cares for us and forgives us and has gone to incredible extremes to rescue us from the fall.

Are there too many noises in your life today? Have you been trying to drown out the emptiness inside?

Please take a moment to listen to the silence of Christ. Hear it echo in your own heart. It is powerful testimony to God's grace. Christ was crushed beneath the weight of sin. He endured the consequences of our indifference to God. And He did it all without a word of complaint or reproach—like a Lamb led to the slaughter.

But what a powerful Savior! What a great Rescuer!

Have you caught a glimpse of the God who has gone to the uttermost lengths to save you? Are you ready for His peace to replace your emptiness?

Why not make a commitment right now at the beginning of the 21st century? Reach out right now, and accept the gracious gift of forgiveness that Christ offers. You don't have to jump off a cliff; you just need to take a step of faith. It's only the peace of Christ that can fill your life to overflowing.

Can You Protect Your Family?

Most people have tried to make their home a refuge from the stresses and strains of life out in the cold, hard world. They've tried to make it a place of love and safety.

But futurists tell us that the home is headed for some pretty dramatic changes. And families will have to adjust. It's more than a matter of Ozzie and Harriet simply getting laptops. The real question is how will family values survive in the 21st century?

What will life be like in your home in the 21st century? How will things be different? What will remain the same? And how will this affect your ability to make the home a healthy, nurturing place for your family?

Well, the first thing we hear from those who've been studying trends sounds like good news. Most futurists agree that people will actually spend much more time at home in the 21st century. More and more activities will be centered at home.

In the decades at the end of the 20th century, the family home almost became a way station to somewhere else. Mom and Dad often worked outside the home, and single parents almost always had to. Parents and kids always seemed to be rushing through. They stopped for a quick bite to eat, or a change of clothes, and then hurried off to a soccer match or a late meeting at the office.

But in the future, many more people will be able to do their work right at home, right at their computer. They'll be connected via the Internet to a wide assortment of new businesses. More and more individuals will become freelance workers and entrepreneurs.

In the next few decades, people will also do more and more of their shopping at home. They'll be able to surf the Net for all kinds of goods and services, order catalogues, conduct transactions, make purchases all right at their keyboard. Television, telephone, computing, information all these things will combine into one interlocking system right in your house.

So, it looks like the home will be alive and well in the 21st century. That's the good news.

But, there's also troubling news. And that relates to how easily unhealthy stuff can get into your home. There will be more and more avenues for incoming material that's dangerous or immoral.

Recently, we've seen examples of how quickly a virus or a hoax can spread to millions on the Internet. Even worse things can spread, too.

Kids can access the most debasing kind of pornography on the Internet.

Disturbed individuals can try to get a family member's name and address through e-mail.

Hate groups and bizarre cults are finding the Internet a great way to spread their propaganda. Any wacko can now have a website.

In the years ahead, popular culture will become a louder and louder voice in our homes and make a bigger picture.

We'll soon be looking at high-definition television screens that fill an entire living room wall. The images will look as sharp as photographs. Gorgeous images will dazzle us and seem to fill the whole room.

But what about the content? What about the messages that

hit us so forcefully?

Listen to one Gen-Xer named Greg. As a nervous newly-wed, he said this: "If you flip on the TV you don't see families anymore. Family life is not part of the canon. It takes a lot of faith to reinstate marriage into your vision of life."

Many young people can only see packaged sport figures and rock stars as role models. They are flooded with MTV-like, rapid-fire, mass-media entertainment. There's only now. Everything's fluid. There are no clear values to hang on to.

That's a cause for concern in the 21st century.

Dr. Shervert Frazier serves as director of the National Institutes of Mental Health. He expressed concerns in his book, *Psychotrends*. Dr. Frazier described what he called a "co-violent society." That's one which "celebrates mayhem while simultaneously condemning it." It ends up making violence seem amoral and inevitable.

In other words, the 6:00 P.M. news shows us a tragic picture of some kid felled on the streets in a drive-by shooting. There's nothing pretty about that at all.

But then the 8:00 P.M. movie shows us a hero mowing down or blowing up the bad guys in some new, spectacular, heart-stopping way. And that's entertainment. Soon it will splash all over your living room wall in living color.

In the 21st century, pop culture will give us more and more of the artistic equivalent of junk food. Radio shock-jocks are already dominating the airwaves, pushing the envelope in ever more crude and vulgar ways.

Daytime TV talk shows try to out-sensationalize each other. They compete for guests with the sickest, most twisted personal lives. Even the traditional news media seems more and more driven by tabloid journalism.

We live in a world in which different values compete for our attention, and for our loyalty. It's pretty much an open marketplace. Your kids will see all kinds of beliefs and practices modeled in the programming that fills those high-definition TV screens. They'll be exposed to many different versions of right and wrong.

So one very important part of protecting your family is helping them make good choices, helping them be able to sort out values. They need to see for themselves the difference between healthy and unhealthy, between moral and immoral.

The question is, how do you make your values count when so many others are bouncing off the wall? How do you do that now? How will you do it in the 21st century?

Now, let's think about helping your family make wise choices. Let me suggest that you start with a vitally important perspective. It's a certain message in the Bible that relates, specifically, to the end times. And, I believe, it provides a background for sorting out right from wrong.

We find it in the book of Revelation. It's the proclamation of three angels given in chapter 14: "Then I saw another angel flying in the midst of heaven, having the everlasting gospel to preach to those who dwell on the earth to every nation, tribe, tongue, and people saying with a loud voice, `Fear God and give glory to Him, for the hour of His judgment has come; and worship Him who made heaven and earth, the sea and springs of water'" (Revelation 14:6, 7 NKJV).

This angel is introducing God's final message to a world hurling toward a rendezvous with destiny, toward the end of time. It certainly bears listening to as we enter the 21st century.

This angel has the "everlasting gospel" to preach to every person on Earth. That's the good news of God's grace, of what Christ accomplished on the cross through His sacrificial death.

And this angel who proclaims the gospel makes this specific call: " 'Fear God, give glory to Him, because the hour of His judgment has come.' "

God is about to judge the world. He's about to judge every individual on the planet. A day of reckoning is upon us. And God has a very clear standard on which He bases judgments of right and wrong.

Paul, in his letter to the Galatians, identifies those who fall under judgment: "Everyone who does not continue in all things which are written in the book of the law, to do them" (Galatians 3:10, NKJV).

God's law—God's commandments—are the unchanging standard of right and wrong. That is the standard in the judgment. And that is what we need to acknowledge as our standard. We are accountable before God for our behavior. We are responsible for our choices.

But we've been losing that perspective. This truth about God's righteous judgment has been disappearing among Christians in recent years. Believers don't want to talk about it too much. Many don't want to think about it at all.

And the truth is, part of the reason we're struggling to protect our families is that we've been running away from God's judgment for so long. Part of the reason we find it hard to help them make wise choices, wise moral choices, is that we've been running away from God's law for so long.

We only want to talk about the gospel. We haven't realized how the judgment and the law are part of the gospel. The whole point of Christ's dying on the cross was to "justify" us in the judgment, to justify us before God's law. God's moral requirements loom large in the drama of salvation.

But we've lost sight of that. And we've lost this sense of accountability before a holy God. We've lost this sense that there's a great standard for behavior. There's something to measure our lives against.

We live in a time when everyone is making up their own rules, when everyone is looking for the truth only in their own hearts. And that comes across over and over in the programming that often fills our homes. It will hit us over and over in the 21st century.

So we need something big to counter that kind of thinking. We need something that will reinforce a different perspective. Well, folks, the final judgment is big enough. That's an event big enough to fill the horizon. And it's an important event that tells us that our actions are measured against the absolute standard of God's law. It's an important event that helps us make wise, moral choices.

Let's say your child has just watched a TV show in which the very cool main character uses a very clever deception to get what he wants. Maybe he pretends to be the star quarterback at school to get the pretty girl he's after, when he's only the water boy. Maybe he sneaks off with his dad's expensive sports car and passes it off as his own.

If your child watches enough of these episodes he or she may begin to wonder: *Maybe I'd get further ahead if I was a little more "creative" with the truth. Maybe honesty isn't all it's cooked up to be.*

Well, if this youngster doesn't have a clear sense of accountability before God, it will be much easier to begin making up his own rules. If he doesn't understand that all we do is measured against the standard of God's law, it won't be hard to rationalize a few lies here and there to get ahead.

But that won't be easy if this young person knows that a holy God accepts and loves him, if he knows that this God wants the best for him, if he knows that this best is spelled out in God's commandments.

Here's the bottom line. The judgment makes God's law bigger; it makes it bigger in our minds. You want your family members to choose God's values when there are many other values competing for attention. The judgment helps make God's values vivid. They're what we all need to be aiming for. They're what Christ fulfilled, at great cost. They're what God is calling us toward.

That's a perspective we badly need in the 21st century. We need this bigger picture; we need it as moral values shrink all around us.

Here's an example of one simple principle from the Word of

God that is part of the big picture. It relates to how values are shaped, and it's never been more relevant. "But we all, with unveiled face, beholding as in a mirror the glory of the Lord, are being transformed into the same image" (2 Corinthians 3:18, NKJV).

We are transformed by beholding, by constant looking. We become what we look at. What our mind habitually focuses on, will begin to mold us. It will mold us for good or for bad.

Think of that terrible tragedy in Littleton, Colorado. Two teenagers walked into their high school one day, loaded with bombs and weapons, and proceeded to shoot down their classmates; as many as they possibly could.

In the shock that followed, we all wondered: how could these youngsters engage in such cold-blooded, merciless killing? How could they laugh as the bodies sprawled around them? How could two teenagers have become so desensitized, so untouched by the suffering of others?

Well, do you know what these boys were doing in the weeks and months before the tragedy? They were playing a violent video game called "Doom" every afternoon. They'd become obsessed with it. The object of the game is to see who can rack up the most "kills."

The two boys also watched a movie called "Natural Born Killers" over and over. It's a depiction, in graphic detail, of a couple engaging in random murders.

Now, everyone who plays violent video games doesn't go out and mow down their classmates. Everyone who watches "Natural Born Killers" doesn't go on a killing spree.

But it's now pretty clear that these things have a serious effect. They're certainly part of the culture of violence in America. And they certainly seem to have affected two troubled kids in Littleton who felt isolated and who wanted revenge.

If you've been blowing people away in a video game day after day, if you've been racking up kills in simulated fire fights day after day, then you're going to become more comfortable, on some level, with killing. It's not hard to see how you could become desensitized to the horror of it all.

We are changed by what we behold. It's not always a dramatic change. It usually takes time. But we are changed by what we behold.

So how can we protect our families? By giving them good things to behold. By helping them feed their minds on what is healthy.

Listen to this wonderful bit of advice from the apostle Paul. "Finally brethren, whatever things are true, whatever things are noble, whatever things are just, whatever things are pure, whatever things are lovely, whatever things are of good report, if there is any virtue and if there is anything praiseworthy meditate on these things" (Philippians 4:8, NKJV).

Meditate on these things. Think on these things. Why? Because by beholding we become changed. Behold what is true, and you'll become more honest. Behold what is just, and you'll become more fair. Behold what is admirable, and you'll become more trustworthy.

There are so many good things we can focus on. So many great books, so many wonderful songs, so much that is honest and genuine and excellent. Fill your home with good things.

It's not enough to just try to keep the bad outside. You've got to get good things inside. You've got to give your kids something better to look at, something better to feed on.

A young man named Richard found himself flat on his back one day, staring at the ceiling of a sanitarium. A very contagious disease had laid him low. And Richard wasn't accustomed to lying low. He'd made quite a reputation for himself at the hottest clubs downtown. He was a player. He always got the flashiest girls. He always flashed the biggest bills.

But now, in the hospital, Richard had only time on his hands. So, out of sheer boredom, he began reading a Bible someone had left for him. He began reading about Jesus Christ, a Person he knew very little about. And Richard was overwhelmed. He couldn't help but compare his own pathetically limited life with Christ's. His own mind was filled with nothing but sensations, it seemed. Christ's every thought was filled with such nobility.

Richard kept reading more and more, filling his mind with this completely different Person, who described such a completely different life. He felt captured by Christ's courage and love. He finally had something better to look at, something much better.

And that changed Richard's life. When he walked out of that hospital, he was a new man. He stopped exploiting women. He wanted his life to count for something big. Richard eventually became a much beloved counselor. He often worked with the poor and those whom life had beaten down. Richard had a gift for helping the most oppressed individuals to feel a measure of dignity and hope again.

He'd found something good that filled his mind. And his life was transformed.

Friends, we can't build a wall high enough to protect our families from unhealthy influences. They are going to have to make choices between different values. But what we can do is give them a bigger picture of God's law. We can teach them about grace and acceptance and about God's ideals. We can teach them about God writing His law within their hearts. We can teach them about forgiveness and grace and love and honor. We can teach them about things that are excellent and praiseworthy.

That's the ultimate goal. That's what will keep our families safe in the long run. Let's commit ourselves to work toward that end.

The Ultimate Space Journey

As we journey into a new century and a new millennium, many people are wondering just how far we will journey into space. Will we find life out there somewhere? Will we find signs of intelligence?

In the next millennium, some see us engaging in interstellar trade, sending out the fruits of the earth in exchange for curios from the stars of the Trapezium, or for jewels from glittering Polaris.

Just how far will human beings be traveling? And will we ever find an ultimate destination?

Space definitely beckons us in the 21st century. After the Apollo missions to the moon concluded in the 1970s, there was a bit of a letdown. We'd explored a heavenly body. We'd brought back rocks. The adventure seemed over.

But now, momentum is gathering for greater journeys. We've already sent probes out to the distant planets in our own solar system. We're building a permanent space station.

And now, NASA's chief says, their goal is to "blacken the sky with spacecraft." These craft will be designed for very specific missions.

One, named Stardust, is set to travel 242 million miles and fly through the path of a particular comet, named Comet

Wild-2. A giant arm, which looks a bit like a fly swatter, will extend to capture icy dust and organic compounds from the comet.

Then there's the planned launch of "Deep Space 4." It will aim for a comet 233 million miles from Earth. The spacecraft will shoot out a harpoon that can anchor itself in the comet. Then a drill will begin digging in to extract something scientists have never seen before: the comet's frozen core.

Another probe will be sent toward Jupiter's moon, Europa. Astronomers think that Europa is completely covered by an ocean, an ocean 60 miles deep with a crust of ice. The probe will melt a hole in the ice and then deploy a submarine to explore those unknown waters.

And then, of course, there are the big dreams. Dreams of building spaceships that can approach the speed of light. Dreams of traveling to other galaxies. Dreams of taking shortcuts in order to cross the immense distances of interstellar space—perhaps sailing into a black hole in order to disappear in one place and reappear instantly in another.

The universe is definitely beckoning at the turn of the 21st century. Movie phenomena like the "Star Wars" series are just one example of our fascination with space. We want to see what's out there. We want to take the ultimate journey. Some private companies are already booking seats on space shuttles planned to shoot far out into orbit.

But it's interesting to note one of the main reasons that we keep reaching out beyond our world. It's interesting to discover why billions of dollars are being invested in those space probes aimed at comets and moons and other planets.

Scientists want to answer this big question: where did we come from? They want to sample a comet's dust trail; they want to drill into its icy core; they want to dive beneath the surface of Europa—to find out about our origins.

All those probes are sent out to discover just what various heavenly bodies are composed of. Scientists hope this will offer clues to how the universe began.

So all these journeys out into space are really journeys back to the beginning of time. We go out to go back. Human beings want to know about the beginning, about where we've come from. That is really the ultimate destination—the discovery of who we are.

In this chapter, I want to tell you about a space journey that will answer that big question, once and for all. It's the ultimate space journey. And it's a journey not just reserved for the elite, for a few astronauts. It's a journey each one of us can take. And it will bring us face to face with who we are.

What's more, we don't have to build a warp-speed space ship in order to make this journey. But deliverance is coming to us. We will journey through space.

Look at these words from the apostle Paul. He was one of the first to receive confirmation about this ultimate journey. And he passed on the good news to the Thessalonians.

In 1 Thessalonians, chapter four, he writes to them. Listen carefully to what is being described: "For if we believe that Jesus died and rose again, even so God will bring with Him those who sleep in Jesus. For the Lord Himself will descend from heaven with a shout, with the voice of an archangel, and with the trumpet of God. And the dead in Christ will rise first. Then we who are alive and remain shall be caught up together with them in the clouds to meet the Lord in the air. And thus we shall always be with the Lord" (1 Thessalonians 4:14, 16, 17, NKJV).

Jesus Christ, the Messiah, the One who paid such a remarkable visit to this planet 2,000 years ago, is going to pay us another visit. And He is going to make quite an entrance the second time.

The heavens will rumble with a great shout as trumpets

blast and angels sing out. Other texts fill in many more details. Every human eye is going to see this spectacle as an army of angelic beings descends through the skies. The face of the coming Christ will shine like the sun at high noon. His garments flash a brilliant white.

Christ and the heavenly host swoop down in a cloud of glory and hover over the surface of the earth like an enormous space ship. The ground shakes. Lightning flashes. Mountains tumble into the sea. And graves split open. Those who've died in Christ rise up, alive. Living believers rise with them—right up into the air, drawn toward this heavenly light. They are drawn into it, drawn in to meet a resplendent Jesus Christ.

And what happens next? Remember how this passage began: "God will bring with Him . . ." He'll bring believers with Him. Bring them where? He'll bring them from Earth to heaven.

Jesus promised us in John: "And if I go and prepare a place for you, I will come again and receive you to Myself; that where I am there you may be also" (John 14:3, NKJV).

That's what is going to happen to all those who've placed their faith in Christ. We are going to be swept up to heaven in that interstellar cloud. We're going to take a journey—so we can always be with the Lord. We are going to take a journey—to the place where Christ has been preparing many mansions. We are going to take a journey—to our Father's house.

Friends, this is the ultimate journey. It's the journey to the center of the universe, to the home of God. Talk about discovering where we've come from! Talk about exploring our origins! This formation of angels is going to take us to our Creator. It's going to take us to the place where all our questions are answered, where our deepest longings are fulfilled.

Let me tell you about another reason behind NASA's big

budget for space exploration. This is another big reason we'll be sending out so many probes at the beginning of the 21st century. Scientists are hoping to find life out there. Maybe some organism will be found deep in that ocean on Europa, Jupiter's moon. Maybe some sign of carbon-based life will show up in the core of a comet.

A couple of years ago, one NASA official made this statement, "In the next 10 to 20 years, we're going to find the potential habitable planets within 100 light-years from us."

Sounds ambitious!

In fact, a whole new science has blossomed around this quest: the science of astrobiology. It uses many different disciplines to try to identify life in the universe. Most scientists don't expect to find a cuddly creature like "ET" any time soon.

But they are looking for one-celled organisms that might be able to survive harsh environments. Life is hardier than we used to assume. We've now discovered certain bacteria that can actually survive, and thrive, in glacial ice and in 250-degree heat under the sea.

Human beings are curious about life out there among the stars. We can't help wanting to make contact somehow. Who knows what we might find? Who knows what intelligent being might start talking back to us?

Well, I have good news about life out there among the stars. We're going to find it. I have good news about signs of intelligence in the universe. It's going to start talking back—in a very big way.

We're going to hear the voice of our Creator echoing over our planet. We're going to hear the voices of angelic beings rumbling across the sky like thunder. We're going to have a cosmic rendezvous.

That's the great event which Christ's disciples tell us is coming. It's much more significant than finding bacteria on Europa. It's more mind-boggling than locating signs of life on a distant planet.

We are going to come face to face with the Greatest Intelligence in the universe. His countenance is going to shine down on this world like the sun at high noon.

Yes, Jesus is going to make a very big entrance—the second time. Listen to this description in Matthew, chapter 24: "For as the lightning comes from the east and flashes to the west, so also will the coming of the Son of Man be. . . . The stars will fall from heaven, and the powers of the heavens will be shaken. . . . Then all the tribes of the earth . . . will see the Son of Man coming on the clouds of heaven with power and great glory. And He will send His angels with a great sound of a trumpet, and they will gather together His elect from the four winds, from one end of heaven to the other" (Matthew 24:27, 29-31, NKJV).

Jesus Christ is going to appear above us, flashing from horizon to horizon. His great angelic space ship of light will make heaven and earth tremble. And He will gather believers, living and dead, from every corner of the planet. He beckons them up toward Him. He beckons them on a journey.

Oh yes, signs of intelligent life in the universe are going to appear. The sign of the Son of God is going to appear. His glory is going to fill the sky.

And everyone who has placed their faith in Jesus Christ is going to be able to journey with Him through the stars, through the galaxies, toward heaven. We will be traveling with the Son of God, Jesus—in whom are hidden all the treasures of wisdom and knowledge.

You know, when we human beings try to think about *real* space travel, about journeying from one galaxy to the next, the huge distances are overwhelming. How do you reach a star thousands of light years away? Scientists today can't conceive of traveling faster than the speed of light.

Some writers have imagined creating a kind of space ark,

a huge vessel built inside a hollowed-out asteroid. It would be sent across space as a self-contained little world with its own population. People would live in it for many generations, taking thousands of years to reach their destination.

But finally, the great-great-great-grandchildren of the original travelers would make it to some distant planet.

Think about this, however. What if people back on Earth develop better technology and much faster ships in the meantime? What if those ships are sent out to the same destination? And what if the great-great-great-grandchildren on that asteroid arrive at last, only to find that others have arrived centuries ahead of them?

Real space travel faces huge obstacles. But the Second Coming of Jesus Christ is going to remove all those obstacles. The One who created all these stars and calls them all by name and leads them forth—this God is capable of moving us through the universe as He pleases.

We'll be flying along with Christ in that angelic formation. Distances won't matter. Black holes won't matter. Even the speed of light won't be a barrier. It's God who beckons us home. And that's all that matters. We will all arrive safely home. And we will all arrive together. We'll all stand together on a sea of glass around the throne of God—and sing our hearts out in exultation.

That's the ultimate space journey. And you know, people at the beginning of the 21st century are becoming more and more aware that we *need* to take some kind of journey; we need to find something beyond this world.

Why? Because we're using up many natural resources on this planet. Experts have begun to look for new supplies out in space. Some talk of mining asteroids for valuable minerals. Listen to this: companies have already started laying down plans to strip-mine the moon. Silicon exists in moon soil in very high concentrations. And there's also plenty of iron there.

This planet is wearing out. It's weighed down with so many problems. People are looking for solutions in other heavenly bodies. Maybe somehow, somewhere in the vast universe, there's a solution to war and hunger and greed. Maybe we can find a better place.

The good news from the Bible is this: that better place is coming here; it's coming down to Earth. It's coming to change things for good.

Now, there's one end-time event that you may not have heard about before. It happens after we've traveled with Christ to heaven. It is the last act in the drama.

We're going to take another incredible space journey. This time, our space ship is going to be an entire city, a city that gleams with golden streets and pearly gates.

Here's what John the apostle saw in vision. It's recorded in Revelation, chapter 21: "And I saw a new heaven and a new earth. . . . Then I, John, saw the holy city, New Jerusalem, coming down out of heaven from God, prepared as a bride adorned for her husband. And I heard a loud voice from heaven saying, 'Behold, the tabernacle of God is with men, and He will dwell with them'" (Revelation 21:1-3, NKJV).

An entire city is going to make an appearance in the sky. And Revelation 20:9 tells us that "the saints," believers, are inside that "beloved city," the New Jerusalem. They've just made another incredible journey through space. They've arrived back on Earth again. It's now time for "a new heaven and a new earth." This world of sin and suffering is cleansed by fire. The scars are gone. The ugliness disappears. The world is born again.

And this New Jerusalem settles down on the planet. Here's where we will live. Here's where God will live with us. We will colonize this renewed planet in an eternal city.

And you know what? The transparent gold of the New Jerusalem's streets won't wear out. Its gates made of enormous pearls won't fall off their hinges. The sapphires and emeralds in the city's foundations won't be used up.

The citizens of the New Jerusalem will be refreshed forever by the River of Life flowing through that city. They will be forever renewed by the Tree of Life in that city, which bears 12 different fruits.

This is the picture in Revelation. And this picture assures us that we are going to find a forever home of peace and blessing. God Himself will become our eternally renewable resource. God Himself will light up that city with His everlasting glory.

I want to take that ultimate journey with God. I want to take that great space odyssey. There's got to be more than mining minerals on the moon. There's got to be more than poking around on asteroids. We need a bigger answer for the longing in our hearts when we look up at the stars. We need a bigger sign of life.

And the Bible tells us, Yes, it's coming. It's coming. Jesus is going to make a spectacular appearance, the second time.

You want to be ready for that event. You want to know this Being who will flash from horizon to horizon. You want to place your faith in the One who will answer back with a voice that thunders across the sky.

You want to be ready for the ultimate space journey.

It's coming. One day you will be swept up into the air and into Christ's arms.

It's coming. One day you will journey to heaven in that angelic craft of light.

It's coming. One day you will journey back through space in a golden city.

It's coming. One day you will live in the earth made new with God.

It's coming. So be ready.

It's coming. So look up.

It's coming. So reach out to the One who is preparing a place for you in His Father's house. Reach out right now.

Information Overload

Sometimes we're so busy making connections—we miss the most important connection.

There is one thing that the 21st century promises to give us in abundance, one thing we can know we'll have plenty of—and that's information. The ways we can receive and send information have multiplied. And new methods of communication have taken a quantum leap in the amount of information that can be stored and transmitted.

Super-computers keep crunching data more and more quickly—and spitting out the megabytes a lot faster than you can bite, much less digest, all the information.

But even that's not enough. People are now looking to photons—particles of light—as the new workhorse of the new millennium. That's because electrons, particles of electronic energy that make possible everything from telephones to computers, seem to be kind of slow these days. You can't push them through copper wires fast enough to keep up with the demands of the Internet.

The traffic on the Information Superhighway is getting heavy. And it will get a lot heavier as things like video-conferencing kick in. We need more lanes.

Well, the photon, this particle of light, can carry data more efficiently. So companies are spending billions to use it on the

Information Superhighway. Fiber-optic cables are vastly increasing what phone lines can carry. It seems that load-carrying ability, or bandwidth, is like closet space—you can never have too much of it.

One company announced a new 80-channel technology; it's capable of sending 400 billion bits of information in one second—over one tiny pipeline of fiber. That's the equivalent of more than 11,000 encyclopedia volumes in one second.

Yes, the flood of information just keeps speeding up. On a personal level, that can be overwhelming. We go home, and there are 12 messages on the answering machine—and we haven't answered all the calls on our beeper, and the fax has been going, and e-mail has been pouring in, and let's not forget all the stuff that's come in the regular mail!

The information always piles up much faster than we can absorb it. And it has more and more ways of getting to us, grabbing us through our cell phone as we drive, beeping us in a restaurant—or even in church.

It's hard to get away from all the information, all the urgent, important information. A lot of people these days have begun to feel they've been run over on the Information Superhighway. It's too much. In the roar of the traffic they can hardly hear themselves think.

And people need a way to stop—a way to stop and process things. We have this sense that we aren't feeling our lives go by, and we're losing the big picture, because everything is speeding by so fast; we can catch only snatches.

People today are suffering from information overload. It's not just that we want to know less. It's that we want it to mean more. We want things to make sense. We don't want to just be swept along in the current of more and more messages, newer and newer things, faster and faster data.

People today want to send out an SOS. It's an SOS for less.

So how do we slow down time? How do we get more meaning amid this flood of information?

I'd like to suggest that our Creator has provided us with the perfect antidote to information overload. It's a gift God gave us some time ago. But it's something that many people have been rediscovering in the last decades of the 20th century—people like Ray.

Ray is a writer and producer living near Los Angeles who is often caught up in the rush of deadlines and production schedules. Ray has to process a great deal of information in his work and, he says, "Sometimes it's just too much. You get a bit numb after a while. You're taking in more and more, but it means less and less."

But Ray has discovered an oasis in the midst of the nonstop rush of life, an oasis that still refreshes at the beginning of the 21st century. It's called Sabbath rest. It's the holy day of rest that God instituted at Creation.

This is how Ray describes it: "In recent years, I've really seen how the Sabbath can affect the quality of my life. When I set this day aside and devote it to God in some way—it's almost like I enter another space. It's a peaceful, nurturing space. There have been times when I felt a bit of heaven coming down to earth during those Sabbath hours. It's been a great interruption to the frantic pace and the mad rush around me."

People are rediscovering the blessings of Sabbath rest: setting the seventh day of the week aside to stop their labors and be with God.

Our Creator actually gave human beings this gift at the very beginning of history, back in the Garden of Eden. Genesis, chapter 2, tells us: "And God blessed the seventh day and made it holy" (Genesis 2:3, NIV).

The God of heaven gave human beings a particular space, a space on the seventh day in which to rest and find spiritual renewal. This Sabbath memorial was later made part of the Ten Commandments in Exodus. The fourth commandment tells us this: "Remember the Sabbath day by keeping it holy. . . . For in six days the Lord made the heavens and the earth . . . but he rested on the seventh day" (Exodus 20:8,11, NIV).

The Sabbath points us back to our Creator, back to our origins, back to who we really are. The book of Deuteronomy gives us another reason for keeping this special day. "Remember that you were slaves in Egypt and that the Lord your God brought you out of there with a mighty hand and an outstretched arm. Therefore the Lord your God has commanded you to observe the Sabbath day." (Deuteronomy 5:15, NIV).

Here the Sabbath memorializes redemption—God saving His people from slavery. Resting on the Sabbath from daily labors symbolizes our rescue from slavery to all kinds of things—slavery to compulsion, slavery to sin. It represents the freedom we can enjoy through resting in God. It represents the bond we can enjoy with God.

In Exodus, the Lord told His people: "You must observe my Sabbaths. This will be a sign between me and you for the generations to come, so you may know that I am the Lord, who makes you holy" (Exodus 31:13, NIV).

The God who makes us holy, the God who renews us, asks us to observe His Sabbaths. Each week they point us to the source of spirituality, to the source of meaning in our lives. Each Sabbath we are reminded of who our God is—our Creator and Redeemer.

Let me share with you some of the specific things Sabbath observance can do in your life. These are some of the reasons people today are re-examining this ancient divine institution. Let's look at just how the Sabbath is God's solution to information overload.

First of all, the Sabbath slows down time by getting us in touch with eternity. It connects us with eternity. On the Sabbath we can pause to reflect.

Let me tell you about a fascinating computer project that helps shed light on this principle.

Danny Hillis has helped design some of the most sophisticated computers in the world. At MIT, he cooked up the idea of massive parallelism—a way to get thousands of microprocessors to work together at once. And he made it happen. Mr. Hillis began taking computers to warp speed. He built a 64,000-processor supercomputer that could do incredible things in mini-seconds.

But then one day near the turn of the 21st century, he woke up and started wondering, "Does the world really need to go faster?" What about centuries? What about millenniums? What about the bigger picture?

Mr. Hillis wanted a way to step back from the endless competitive race for silicon speed. And so he began building what he called a Millennium clock, a monumental device that would keep accurate time for 10,000 years.

He designed a chipless digital calculator that could keep it on track. A quartz lens would focus sunlight to automatically correct any deviations from exact time. This "Clock of Ages" would be made of glass, tungsten, and sapphire, made to last.

Others became interested in the project and started the "Long Now Foundation." Hillis was able to build a prototype. But his big dream is to construct a giant Mountain Clock somewhere in the high desert of California.

He imagines people entering through a tunnel in a cliff and coming upon this huge vertical mechanism. Light breaks through. They look up and see a piece of sky. It's the clock face. It's the full-sized Millennium Clock. It will be ticking away—not the seconds, but the years. One tick annually. And it will chime every thousand years.

That's the idea behind the "Long Now." Mr. Hillis and his colleagues want to slow the rush of time down by getting people in touch with a larger perspective, a bigger picture.

Well, the Sabbath is a much more accessible way to do just that. We don't have to visit a giant clock in a mountain; we just have to experience Sabbath rest.

The Sabbath interrupts the week, stops the week, to remind us of where we've come from—and where we're going. It ties us back to the first week of the world, the week of creation, the week when God rested on the seventh day. It points us toward a future Sabbath rest with God in heaven.

The Sabbath slows down time by getting us in touch with eternity. Worshiping God on this special day gives us that longer perspective, that bigger picture.

Look at this divine promise given through the prophet Isaiah: "Call the Sabbath a delight, the holy day of the Lord honorable. . . . Then you shall delight yourself in the Lord; and I will cause you to ride on the high hills of the earth" (Isaiah 58:13, 14, NKJV).

God wants to take us to high places. He wants to give us a broader perspective. He wants us to see how our lives fit into a bigger picture. But we can't do that if the day-after-day of our busy lives is never interrupted.

Well, the Sabbath is that good interruption which enables us to hear the ticks of eternity, the chimes of God's great plans. The Sabbath slows down time by getting us in touch with eternity.

Now, let's look at the second way in which the Sabbath is God's antidote to information overload.

The Sabbath slows down time by helping us set the right priorities.

Priorities tell us what's important and what's not so important. When you're flooded by an almost unlimited amount of information each day, you need to sort through that information. There's always so much clamoring for your attention. You need a clear idea of what you should pay attention to.

There are always so many things to do; there's always more than you can fit in your schedule. So you need to know what's worth doing, what will really count in the long run.

Without priorities you just get stuck in the flow, swept on by in a sea of messages and demands, never able to quite catch up.

Marketers are aware of something they call "gizmo clutter." People are starting to get a bit weighed down by their high-tech toys.

Take Al, for example, an engineer in Wisconsin. He comes to work each day wearing a pager and cell phone on one side of his belt, and a personal digital assistant on the other that stores his appointments and e-mail. But he's also got an ID card to open the office door, a Timex Data Link watch, and a laptop computer.

Al says, "I feel like I have Batman's utility belt on."

Too much stuff. Too much gizmo clutter.

But as a solution, do you know what people are proposing? More gizmos. Yes, an all-purpose super gadget. They're developing cellular phones now that can also function as hand-held computers. And hand-held computers are taking over the functions of pagers, electronic planners, and calculators.

I'm sure these devices will prove helpful to some people. But they can't help us with the big question—what's important? What is worth concentrating on? What should I ignore?

I'd like to suggest that the Sabbath was designed by our Creator to help us set the right priorities, to help us ask the big questions. That's because it's a time when we strip away all the work, all the duties, all the busyness. It's a time when we concentrate on what matters most—relationships.

We don't need to get connected to more gadgets. We need to get connected to God and to each other.

In one very dark hour of Israel's history, the Hebrews seem to have become completely disconnected from God. They'd been conquered by Babylon. They'd been dragged off into exile. They'd lost sight of who they were. They'd lost sight of what was important.

But the prophet Ezekiel stood up among the exiles, and he issued this challenge from the Lord: " 'I am the Lord your God; follow my decrees and be careful to keep my laws. Keep my Sabbaths holy, that they may be a sign between us. Then you will know that I am the Lord your God' " (Ezekiel 20:19, 20, NIV).

The people of Israel needed to get back to God's principles, God's precepts. That would help them sort out their priorities. That would help them focus on what was important—even after their lives were turned upside down.

And one of God's commands would help them do just that.

"Keep my Sabbaths holy," God said. The Sabbath creates a space each week in which we can stop and reflect. It's a time to look at our lives and sort through things based on God's principles, God's priorities.

The Sabbath can become a sign between you and God. It can become a bonding experience. As you spend this quality time with your Creator, and as you seek to align your life with His principles, you will *know* Him as your Lord; you will experience that closeness which gives you a secure identity.

We don't need more gadgets, friends. We need the right priorities. We need to focus more on relationships and less on things. And that's what the Sabbath can help us do. It slows down time by helping us set the right priorities. It helps us get in touch with our Creator.

Would you like to get into the bigger picture today? Would you like to slow down time in the next century—so you can actually live, instead of just catch up? Would you like to get in touch with eternity? Would you like to set the right priorities?

If you would, I invite you to take advantage of a wonderful gift. Take advantage of the gift that comes to us from Creation. Take advantage of the gift we will enjoy in heaven. Take advantage of the gift that offers a bonding experience with your Creator and Redeemer. Take advantage of the gift of Sabbath rest.

You may think you don't have enough time to dedicate this time to God. Friend, you don't have enough time *not* to do it. You can't afford *not* to slow down. We all need to invest in this most important connection. We all need the blessing of Sabbath rest.

So I invite you to try an experiment. Try to experience the Sabbath as God originally designed it. Make a commitment to observe His Sabbath commandment. And then see what happens in your life. See if you don't get much more out of the rest of the week.

I challenge you to try it. I challenge you to begin the 21st century with the gift that comes to us from the beginning of Creation.

Preserving You
on a Disk

It's sometimes said that you never really feel alone in the world until you stand at your parent's grave. It leaves you without a lifelong cheerleader. It makes you realize you're next in line. And it haunts you with a question, "Can I find hope that goes beyond the grave?"

Tina sat in the hospital at 3:00 A.M. listening to her father's painful gasps. This was the man who'd helped change her diapers and taught her to ride a bike. He'd been a hearty dock worker most of his life. But now cancer had reduced him to a frail, disoriented fragment of himself.

Dad was dying. He couldn't fight any longer.

After the funeral, Tina thought she'd be able to just go on with her life. But nothing is quite the same. She's haunted by the parent who isn't there. She may catch a scent of Old Spice, his aftershave, or hear a Sinatra song he loved, and be overcome with tears.

Tina says, "I know I'm an adult and I'm supposed to be strong. But there are some days I feel like I'm four years old, and all I want is my dad."

Millions of people like Tina are facing one of life's toughest rites of passage—watching a parent die. It's an experience that's going to hit many of us hard as we journey into a new century. The generation born after World War II, the

Baby Boomers, is well into middle age. Statistics tell us that by the time they turn 50, a quarter of the population typically lose their mothers and half lose their fathers.

A parent's death shakes people up. It often leads to depression, family conflict, or a mid-life crisis. And it makes individuals painfully aware of their own mortality.

Boomers are particularly vulnerable. That's because so many of them have given up the religious faith of the mother or father they are laying in the grave.

In the 1950s, in the United States, for example, church going was very much part of family life. That's when Boomers grew up. Their parents, by and large, clung to the strong American tradition of faith, and tried to pass that faith on.

But a lot of things turned upside down in the 60s and 70s. Young people rebelled against what their parents stood for. They wanted to create their own very different values. And often they plunged into drugs, promiscuity and radical politics.

These young people criticized almost everything about what they called "the establishment." And often that included established religion. Church didn't seem very relevant. And many left it behind.

But now, as they kneel by the grave of a father or mother, they are facing big questions. And they don't have good answers. They have lost touch with a faith that could have given them hope beyond the grave.

It's a difficult moment—looking down at that coffin, not having any reason to believe you'll ever see that loved one again, perhaps wondering if some of the values you were so quick to dismiss might not be relevant after all.

A much younger generation often runs into the same difficulty. People in their 20s haven't grown up with many clear values. They don't have a lot of hope about the future. And they would very much like some solid answers about life and death as they head into the 21st century. They would especially like some answers as they lay a grandmother or grandfather in the grave.

In this chapter, I'd like to give you a clear answer to the big question about life after death. I'd like to share with you a very important part of the hope that comes to us out of the New Testament, out of the experience of Christ and His disciples.

This particular answer is part of many other answers that God gives us, answers to the challenges we face as human beings at the turn of a new century.

Now, let's try to get a firm hold on a hope that can stick with us. And let me start with a principle laid down by the apostle Paul.

This man had many close brushes with death. Traveling around the Mediterranean, he survived shipwrecks, imprisonment, attacks by mobs, and murderous plots by religious fanatics. Paul had to be able to look death in the face and still proclaim a gospel filled with hope.

And this is one big reason he did just that. This is how he expressed it in a letter to the Colossians: "For you died, and your life is hidden with Christ in God. When Christ who is our life appears, then you also will appear with Him in glory" (Colossians 3:3, 4, NKJV).

People who place their faith in Jesus Christ as Savior and Lord are given a new identity. They die to the old life, and they find a new life "hidden with Christ in God." Their identity is hidden away, tucked securely away, with Christ in God.

God has such a hold on them in Christ, that when Christ appears gloriously in the heavens they, too, will in some sense "appear with Him in glory."

Here, Paul is giving us an essential principle. This is why hope is possible; this is what it's based on: our life being "hidden with Christ in God." In the New Testament, all kinds of good things happen to human beings because they are "in Christ." And one of those good things is "eternal life."

Paul makes it very plain in Romans, chapter six: "For the wages of sin is death, but the gift of God is eternal life in Christ Jesus our Lord" (Romans 6:23, NKJV).

Eternal life comes to us "in Christ Jesus." It comes to us because our life is "hidden with Christ in God."

But many people are wondering, can we still believe that today, can we still believe it as we enter the 21st century? We don't see direct evidence of eternal life on this earth. All we see is mortal human beings, people who are buried and crumble to dust.

Can we really have a solid hold on the hope of eternal life today? Just how does a person's life become "hidden with Christ in God?"

Well, consider this. It's an almost universal human instinct to hide something away when facing death. Archaeologists uncover that fact all the time. They almost always find artifacts buried with a corpse, precious possessions that are supposed to help an individual in the afterlife, possessions that identify who this individual is.

Human beings have been doing that for thousands of years. We've tried to preserve something of an individual's essence. We've wanted to hide something away with him or her that won't just crumble to dust.

And we're still at it. Only today, we do it in what appears to be more scientific ways. Take cryonics, for example. It's the practice of preserving an individual by freezing his or her body after death. The hope is that some medical breakthrough in the future will permit scientists to thaw out the body and bring that person to life again.

Others speculate about what we might be able to hide away inside tomorrow's computers. We can already store an incredible amount of information on discs and hard drives. What if you could somehow transfer everything that's in someone's mind into megabytes of information in a file? What if you could preserve a personality that way?

In his book *The Next 500 Years*, Adrian Berry included a chapter called "The Search for Immortality." And there he makes an interesting comparison.

Berry writes: "The brain and the mind are just as separate from each other as the computer and its programs which tell it what to do. The brain, like the computer, is 'hardware', while the mind, like programs and files, is 'software' " (p. 82).

What Berry and others like him are implying is that, even if our hardware falls part, even if our brain decays, maybe we can still preserve that software, what's in the mind. Maybe all the ideas and emotions, all the strengths and weaknesses that make up our personality, could be transferred and stored as information. What if all of that could be loaded into another computer, another brain, and live on?

Sounds like science fiction, doesn't it? Well, it's just speculation. But people speculate like this because of this persistent human need, the need to hide something away, to somehow preserve the essence of ourselves. We don't want to be obliterated. We don't want to become a zero—a nothing.

Well, may I suggest that God has designed a way for us never, ever to become a zero. I believe He has devised a plan so that every believer, no matter what happens to the hardware, the body, can be preserved and recreated as a whole personality. God has a way of preserving vital information. And it has to do with that basic principle of our life being hidden with Christ in God.

Let's see exactly what that meant for the apostle Paul. Here's what he was referring to when he talked about believers appearing with Christ in glory.

He spells it out very clearly in 1 Thessalonians: "For the Lord Himself will descend from heaven with a shout, with the voice of an archangel, and with the trumpet of God. And the dead in Christ will rise first. Then we who are alive and remain shall be caught up together with them in the clouds to meet the Lord in the air. And thus we shall always be with the Lord" (1 Thessalonians 4:16, 17 NKJV).

The second coming of Christ brings eternity to Earth. Deceased believers rise from their graves. All rise to meet the glorified Christ. This is the moment when mortality puts on immortality. This is the time when death is swallowed up in victory.

Paul and the other apostles focus their hope of immortality on the second coming of Jesus Christ. Death is a sleep for them. That's what Jesus called it. It's a sleep that Christ will interrupt at His second coming. That's the blessed hope.

But at the same time, we find a few other verses in the New Testament that seem to imply a different hope, or at least a different time frame. And some have interpreted these verses to mean that believers go straight to heaven immediately after death.

The book of Ecclesiastes in the Old Testament describes human death, dust returning to dust, in this way: "Then the dust will return to the earth as it was, and the spirit will return to God who gave it" (Ecclesiastes 12:7, NKJV).

The spirit returns to God. What does that mean?

When the apostle Paul was facing a possible death sentence, he wrote the Philippians that he was hard pressed between two possibilities, remaining in the flesh with his beloved friends, or departing and being with Christ.

When he wrote the Corinthians, Paul pictured the same two options. He said being absent from the body meant being present with the Lord.

Texts like these have tripped some people up. They start

wondering: so just when are we going to heaven? Do we go there at the second coming of Jesus? Many verses say that clearly. Or do we go there right after we die, as some verses seem to imply?

Well, I believe we find an answer to our questions in that basic principle of hope, our lives hidden with Christ in God.

That phrase is true of all believers, living and dead, who have placed their faith in Jesus Christ. Our lives are hidden with Christ in God. Ephesians tells us, in fact, that believers have resurrected with Christ, they have ascended with Him, and they are seated with Christ at God's right hand in heavenly places.

That's our secure position as believers. But that doesn't mean we are physically in heaven. We're still walking around here, driving to work each day, going to bed each night. Our conscious being is still all here on Earth. And the dead, as the New Testament points out, are asleep here on Earth.

But what Paul is saying is that God has a hold of us in a special way. He is holding our essence, our identity, in His hands. And because of that we have hope of eternal life.

When we die, all this hardware is going to go away. All this flesh is going to decay. But, friends, the good news is this: God is going to keep holding on to our identities when we're laid in the ground. He's going to keep holding on to us when dust returns to dust.

How can He do that? Because God has an infinite capacity to store information. He has enough memory. He has enough megabytes to fill the universe. He's the One who designed our original software, the miracle of our unique personality. And he's the One who can preserve it even beyond the grave.

Maybe you've been looking down at the gravestone of a mother or father and feeling lost and alone. Maybe you're grieving the loss of a parent and wondering if you can find big answers to the big questions.

May I suggest that the heavenly Father has what you're looking for. This Parent has gone to great lengths to give you hope. He's gone to great lengths to make eternal life possible for you and your loved ones.

He's the only One who can keep holding on to you after dust returns to dust. He's the only One who doesn't have to let go.

On a flight about to land in Los Angeles, everybody on board was panicking. Something had gone wrong with the hydraulics on the plane, and passengers had to prepare for a crash landing. There were many heart-wrenching sobs as they buckled up tightly and laid their heads on pillows. Many people became hysterical. Even the most seasoned business travelers looked pale as ghosts.

But amid all the noise and confusion, one voice could be heard calmly talking. It was a young mother sitting beside her little girl. She leaned over and said again and again, "Remember how much I love you. Remember how much I love you."

And the child didn't seem to notice the terror in that plane. She just kept looking into her mother's face; she just kept sensing her mother's loving hands on her.

Then, just before the plane touched down, this mother lay down on the seat, covering her child, and buckled the seat belts around them both.

Miraculously, the landing gear held up, and the plane made a safe landing. As the other passengers started weeping with relief, they noticed the mother lying there with her daughter wrapped in her arms, still holding on, holding on to the very end.

That's what God is like. That's what it means for our lives to be hidden with Christ in God. We can be assured that our identity, what makes us who we are, is preserved safely in God's hands.

That's the hope which Bible writers express. That's what it means for our spirits to return to God. That's why Paul could talk about being with Christ even after his death. He was confident that his identity would be preserved in Christ. It would be preserved no matter how long the sleep of death lasted. Even after he'd become dust. Even after every physical trace of Paul had disappeared, after every molecule had been broken down, God still held his identity in His hands; the information was still there. There would be no blips in God's memory.

And Paul knew that God was going to bring him to conscious life again at the second coming of Jesus Christ. All deceased believers would rise from the dead. And they'd rise with new, glorious, perfectly healthy bodies.

All the texts of hope in the New Testament fit together. They all fill in the same picture. We're all going to heaven after the second coming of Jesus Christ.

But the reason we'll be going, the reason we'll be there, is that our lives are hidden with Christ in God. That can be true right now. That can be true at the hour of our death. God is the only One who can hold our identities in His hands. He's the only One who can keep holding on even when we're laid in the grave.

Do you have this wonderful assurance today?

I wouldn't put my faith in a cryonics lab that claims to freeze-dry your brain. I wouldn't put my faith in some supercomputer in the future that might reduce you to gigabytes.

I'd put my faith in a heavenly Father who loves you and gave up His Son so that you could have eternal life. That's who I want holding on to me right now. That's who I want holding on to me at the hour of death.

You can make sure, right now, that your life is hidden with Christ in God. You can have that assurance just by taking a definite step of faith toward God.

FREE Bible Reading Guides

Call toll free
1-800-253-3000
or mail the coupon below
Today!

*B*ecome better
acquainted with your Bible

- *No cost now or in the future.*
- *Designed especially for busy people like you.*
- *Study at home.*
- *These guides will bring the Bible to life.*

☐ **Yes!** Please send me the
26 **FREE** Bible Reading Guides.

Name _____

Address _____

City _____

State/Province _____ Postal Code _____

Please mail this completed coupon to: **DISCOVER**

 it is written • Box O • Thousand Oaks, CA 91360